All-American Ragtime Duets

BY GLENDA AUSTIN

ISBN 978-1-4234-7964-2

WILLIS MUSIC

EXCLUSIVELY DISTRIBUTED BY

Visit Hal Leonard Online at
www.halleonard.com

World headquarters, contact:
Hal Leonard
7777 West Bluemound Road
Milwaukee, WI 53213
Email: info@halleonard.com

In Europe, contact:
Hal Leonard Europe Limited
Dettingen Way
Bury St. Edmunds, Suffolk, IP33 3YB
Email: info@halleonardeurope.com

In Australia, contact:
Hal Leonard Australia Pty. Ltd.
4 Lentara Court
Cheltenham, Victoria, 3192 Australia
Email: info@halleonard.com.au

CONTENTS

The Albuquerque Rag

for the New Mexico Federation of Music Teachers
Albuquerque, New Mexico

SECONDO

Glenda Austin

The Albuquerque Rag

for the New Mexico Federation of Music Teachers
Albuquerque, New Mexico

PRIMO

Glenda Austin

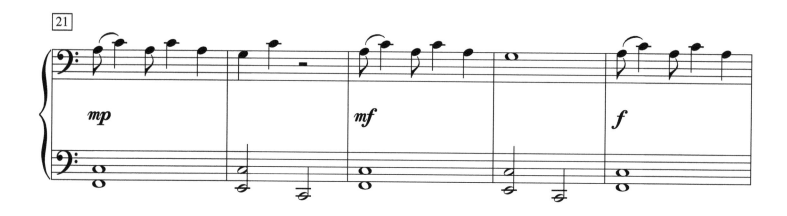

PRIMO

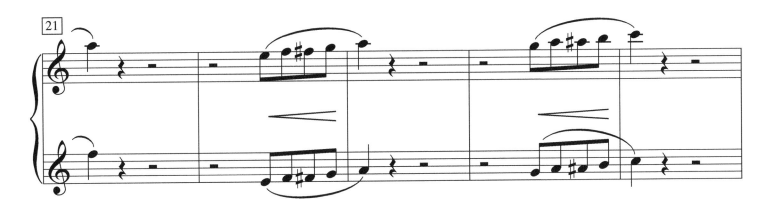

The Joplin Jubilee Rag

in honor of
The Joplin Piano Teachers' Association's 50th Anniversary (2006)
Joplin, Missouri

SECONDO

Glenda Austin

The Joplin Jubilee Rag

in honor of
The Joplin Piano Teachers' Association's 50th Anniversary (2006)
Joplin, Missouri

PRIMO

Glenda Austin

SECONDO

PRIMO

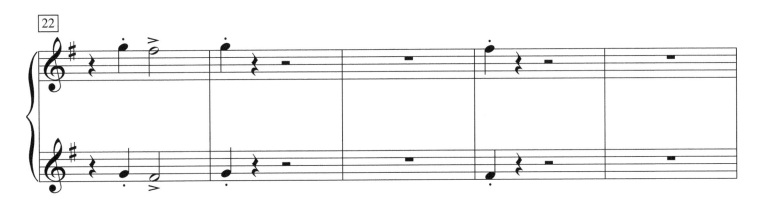

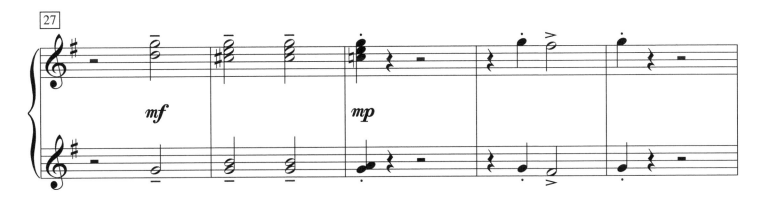

SECONDO

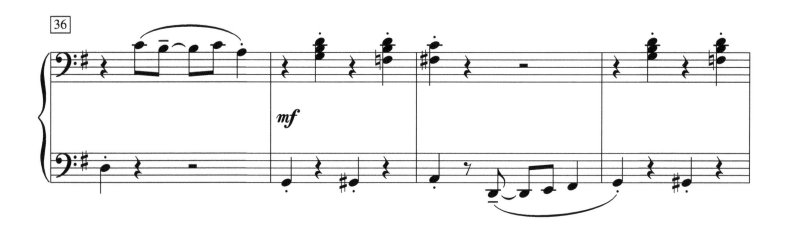

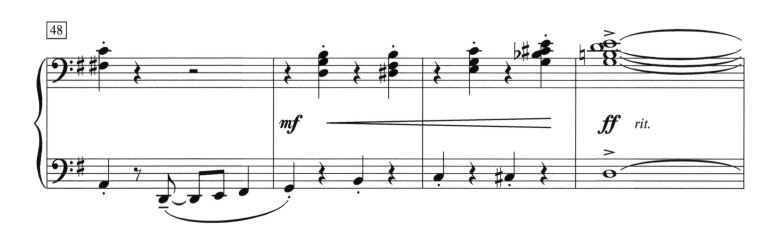

PRIMO

SECONDO

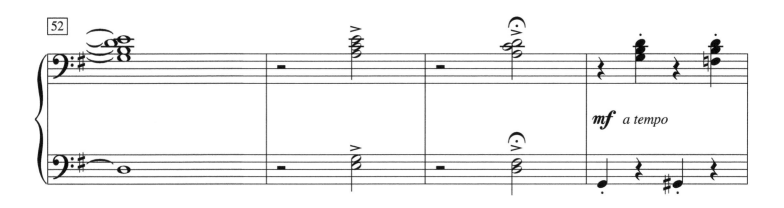

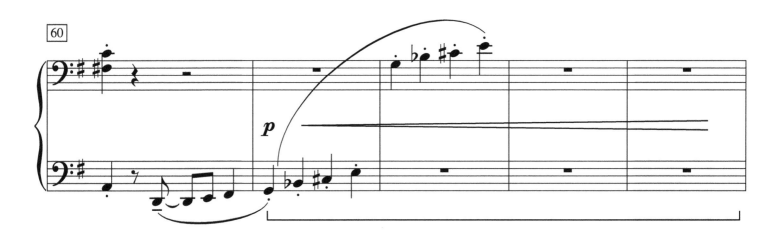

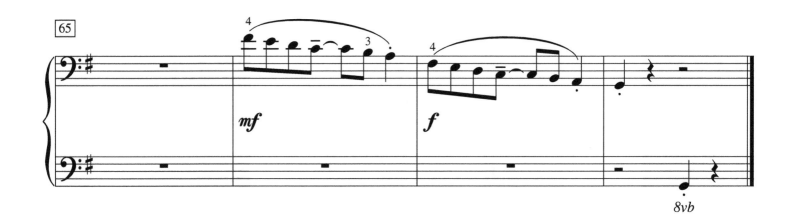

8vb

PRIMO

The Kalamazoo Rag

for the Kalamazoo Area Music Teachers' Association
Kalamazoo, Michigan

SECONDO

Glenda Austin

The Kalamazoo Rag

for the Kalamazoo Area Music Teachers' Association
Kalamazoo, Michigan

PRIMO

Glenda Austin

SECONDO

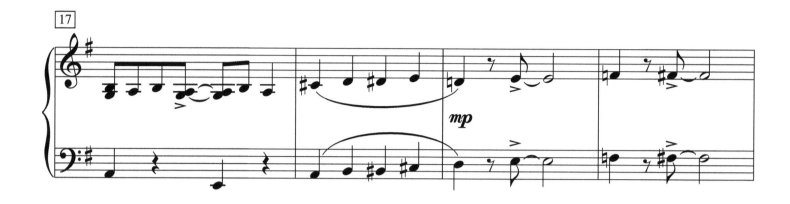

PRIMO

SECONDO

SECONDO

PRIMO

The Kansas City Rag

for the Federated Teachers of Music and Fine Arts, Inc., of Greater Kansas City
Kansas City, Missouri

SECONDO

Words and Music by
Glenda Austin

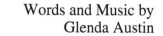

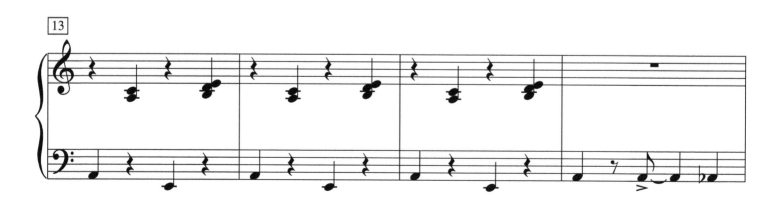

The Kansas City Rag

for the Federated Teachers of Music and Fine Arts, Inc., of Greater Kansas City
Kansas City, Missouri

PRIMO

Words and Music by
Glenda Austin

Not too fast, but very rhythmic

SECONDO

PRIMO

SECONDO

31

PRIMO

SECONDO

CODA

61

65

68 Very slow

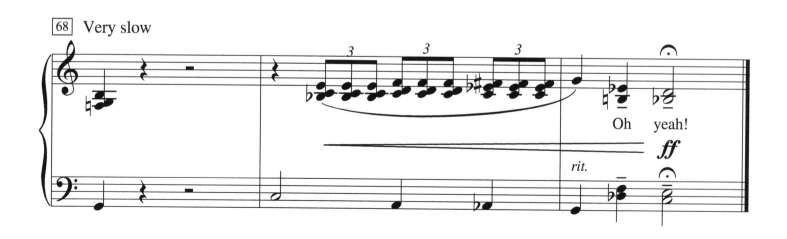

Oh   yeah!

PRIMO

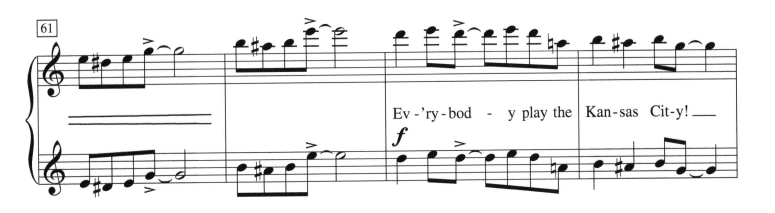

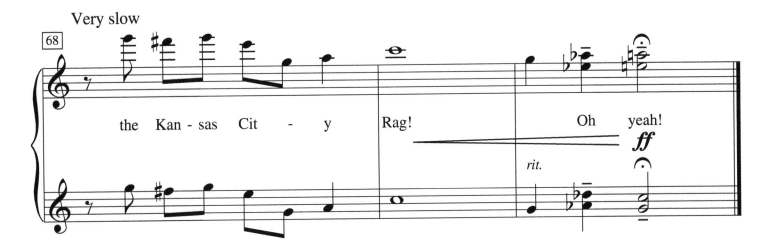

The Omaha Rag

for the Omaha Music Teachers' Association
Omaha, Nebraska

SECONDO

Glenda Austin

Nice and easy, with a bounce *(keep ♩ detached throughout)*

The Omaha Rag

for the Omaha Music Teachers' Association
Omaha, Nebraska

PRIMO

Glenda Austin

Nice and easy, with a bounce *(keep ♩ detached throughout)*

SECONDO

PRIMO

SECONDO

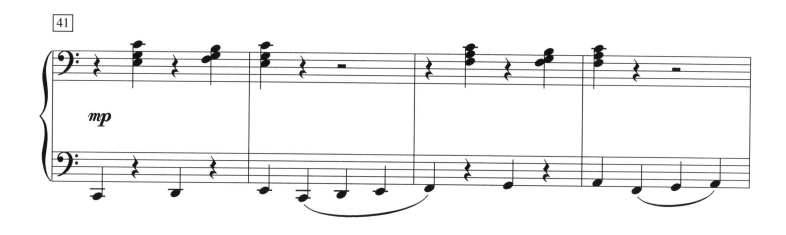

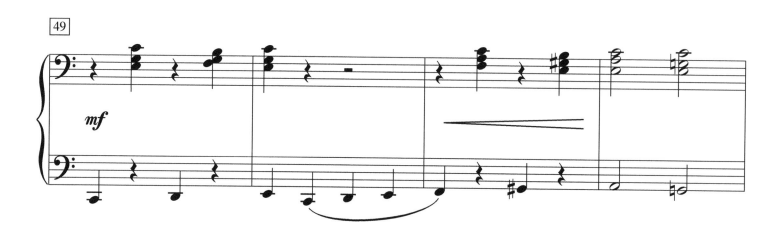

PRIMO

SECONDO

The Texarkana Rag

for the Texarkana Music Teachers' Association
of Arkansas and Texas

SECONDO

Glenda Austin

The Texarkana Rag

for the Texarkana Music Teachers' Association
of Arkansas and Texas

PRIMO

Glenda Austin

SECONDO

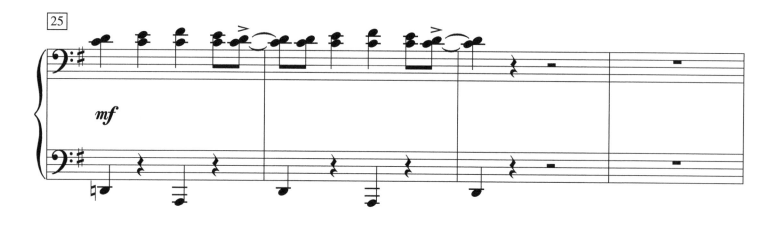

PRIMO

SECONDO

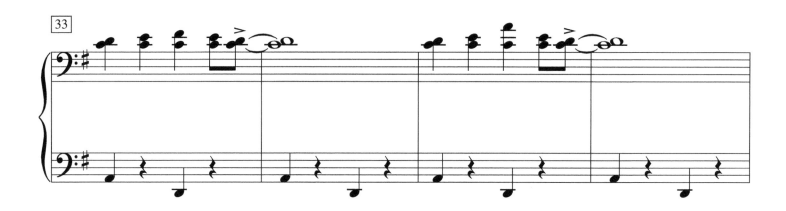

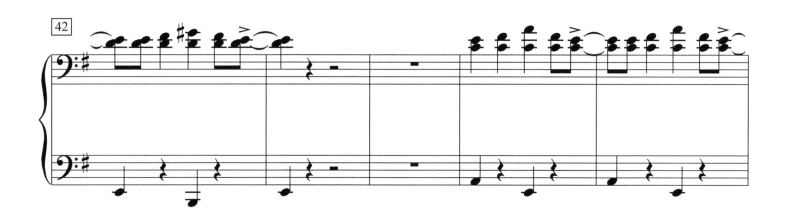

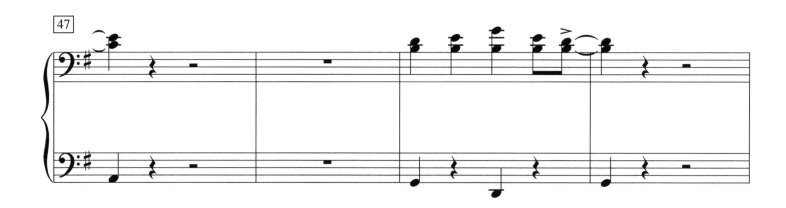

PRIMO

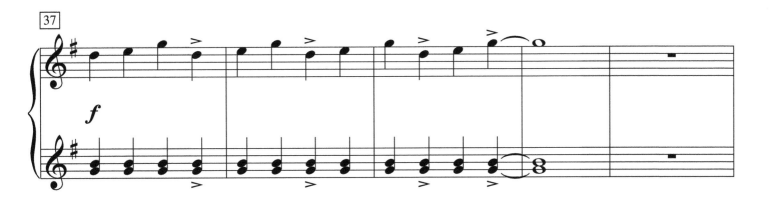

SECONDO

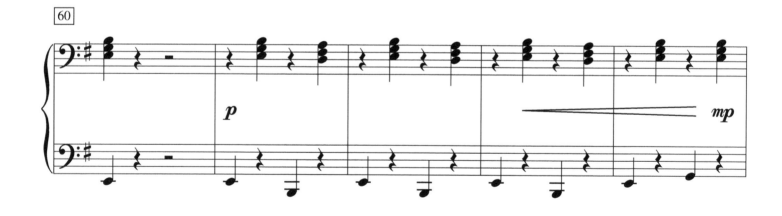

PRIMO

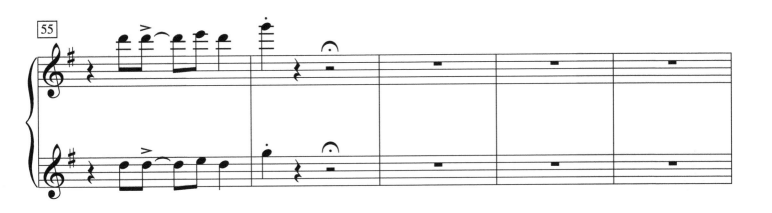

SECONDO

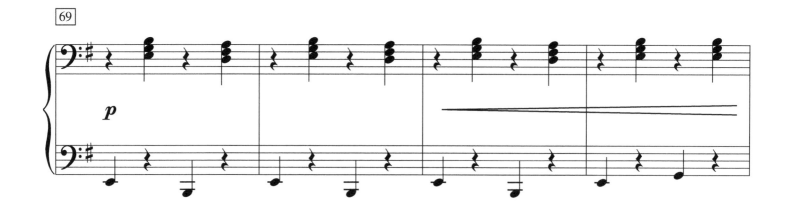

PRIMO

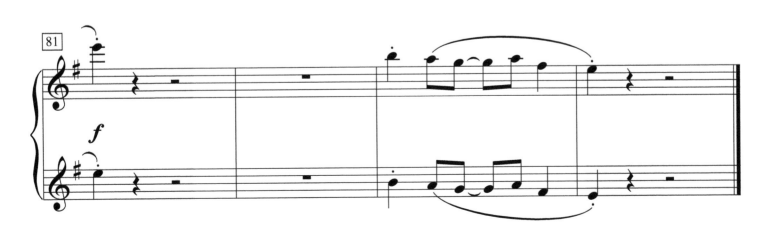

A DOZEN A DAY

by Edna Mae Burnam

The **A Dozen A Day** books are universally recognized as one of the most remarkable technique series on the market for all ages! Each book in this series contains short warm-up exercises to be played at the beginning of each practice session, providing excellent day-to-day training for the student. All book/audio versions include orchestrated accompaniments by Ric Ianonne.

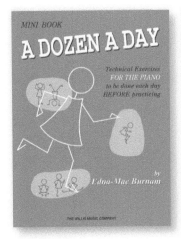

MINI BOOK
00404073 Book Only $6.99
00406472 Book/Audio $10.99

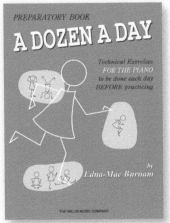

PREPARATORY BOOK
00414222 Book Only $6.99
00406476 Book/Audio $10.99

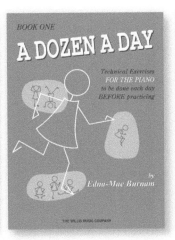

BOOK 1
00413366 Book Only $6.99
00406481 Book/Audio $10.99

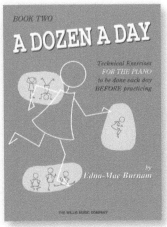

BOOK 2
00413826 Book Only $6.99
00406485 Book/Audio $10.99

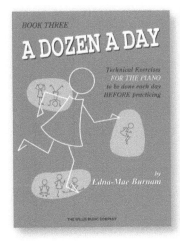

BOOK 3
00414136 Book Only $7.99
00416760 Book/Audio $10.99

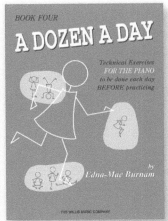

BOOK 4
00415686 Book Only $7.99
00416761 Book/Audio $11.99

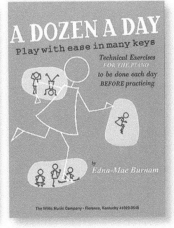

**PLAY WITH EASE
IN MANY KEYS**
00416395 Book Only $6.99

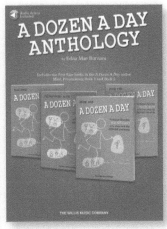

**A DOZEN A DAY
ANTHOLOGY**
00158307 Book/Audio $25.99

ALSO AVAILABLE:
The **A Dozen A Day Songbook** series containing Broadway, movie, and pop hits!

Visit Hal Leonard Online at **www.halleonard.com**

WILLIS MUSIC

EXCLUSIVELY DISTRIBUTED BY

HAL•LEONARD®

Prices, contents, and availability subject to change without notice.
Prices listed in U.S. funds.

MUSIC FROM
William Gillock

Available exclusively from Willis Music

"The Gillock name spells magic to teachers around the world..."
Lynn Freeman Olson, renowned piano pedagogue

NEW ORLEANS JAZZ STYLES

William Gillock's bestselling *New Orleans Jazz Styles* have been repertoire staples since the 1960s. He believed that every student's musical education should include experiences in a variety of popular styles, including jazz, as a recurring phase of study. Because spontaneity is an essential ingredient of the jazz idiom, performers are encouraged to incorporate their own improvisations.

NEW ORLEANS JAZZ STYLES
Mid-Intermediate
New Orleans Nightfall • The Constant Bass • Mardi Gras • Dixieland Combo • Frankie and Johnny (Theme and Variations).
00415931 Book Only $6.99

MORE NEW ORLEANS JAZZ STYLES
Mid-Intermediate
New Orleans Blues • Taking It Easy • After Midnight • Mister Trumpet Man • Bourbon Street Saturday Night.
00415946 Book Only $6.99

STILL MORE NEW ORLEANS JAZZ STYLES
Mid-Intermediate
Mississippi Mud • Uptown Blues • Downtown Beat • Canal Street Blues • Bill Bailey.
00404401 Book Only $6.99

NEW ORLEANS JAZZ STYLES – COMPLETE EDITION
Mid to Late Intermediate
This complete collection features updated engravings for all 15 original piano solos. In addition, access to orchestrated online audio files is provided.
00416922 Book/Online Audio... $19.99

NEW ORLEANS JAZZ STYLES DUETS – COMPLETE EDITION
Early to Mid-Intermediate
arr. Glenda Austin
All 15 pieces from Gillock's classic *New Orleans Jazz Styles* series adapted for piano duet! Includes access to audio files online for practice.
00362327 Book/Online Audio .. $14.99

NEW ORLEANS JAZZ STYLES SIMPLIFIED – COMPLETE EDITION
Late Elementary to Early Intermediate
arr. Glenda Austin
All 15 songs from the *New Orleans Jazz Styles* series adapted for easy piano.
00357095 3 Books in One! $12.99

ACCENT ON... SERIES

ACCENT ON GILLOCK SERIES
Excellent piano solos for recitals in all levels by Gillock.

$5.99 each
00405993 Volume 1
00405994 Volume 2
00405995 Volume 3
00405996 Volume 4

$6.99 each
00405997 Volume 5
00405999 Volume 6
00406000 Volume 7
00406001 Volume 8

Complete Edition
00361225 8 Books in One! $24.99

ACCENT ON... REPERTOIRE BOOKS

00415712 **Analytical Sonatinas** Early Intermediate...... $7.99
00122148 **Around the World** Early Intermediate........ $8.99
00415797 **Black Keys** Mid-Intermediate.................. $5.99
00416932 **Classical** Early to Mid-Intermediate........... $8.99
00415748 **Majors** Late Elementary........................ $6.99
00415569 **Majors & Minors** Early Intermediate.......... $7.99
00415165 **Rhythm & Style** Mid-Intermediate............ $6.99
00118900 **Seasons** Early Intermediate.................... $8.99
00278505 **Timeless Songs** Early Intermediate.......... $12.99

ACCENT ON DUETS
Mid to Later Intermediate
8 original duets, including: Sidewalk Cafe • Liebesfreud (Kreisler) • Jazz Prelude • Dance of the Sugar Plum Fairy (Tchaikovsky) • Fiesta Mariachi.
00416804 1 Piano/4 Hands $13.99

ACCENT ON SOLOS – COMPLETE
Early to Late Elementary
All 3 of Gillock's popular *Accent on Solos* books. These 33 short teaching pieces continue to motivate piano students of every age!
00200896........................... $14.99

ACCENT ON TWO PIANOS
Intermediate to Advanced
Titles: Carnival in Rio • On a Paris Boulevard • Portrait of Paris • Viennese Rondo. Includes a duplicate score insert for the second piano.
00146176 2 Pianos, 4 Hands..... $12.99

ALSO AVAILABLE

CLASSIC PIANO REPERTOIRE – WILLIAM GILLOCK
Elementary
8 great solos have been re-engraved for this collection: Little Flower Girl of Paris • Spooky Footsteps • On a Paris Boulevard • Stately Sarabande • Rocking Chair Blues • and more!
00416957............................. $8.99

CLASSIC PIANO REPERTOIRE – WILLIAM GILLOCK
Intermediate to Advanced
A dozen delightful pieces have been re-engraved in this collection. Includes favorites such as *Valse Etude, Festive Piece, Polynesian Nocturne,* and *Sonatine.*
00416912........................... $12.99

LYRIC PIECES
Early Intermediate
Most of these wonderfully warm and lyrical short pieces are one-page long. Includes: Drifting Clouds • Homage to Chopin • Intermezzo • Land of Pharaoh • A Memory of Paris • Petite Etude • Summer Clouds • and more.
00405943............................. $7.99

WILLIAM GILLOCK RECITAL COLLECTION
Intermediate to Advanced
Features an extensive compilation of over 50 of William Gillock's most popular and frequently performed recital pieces. Newly engraved and edited to celebrate Gillock's centennial year.
00201747................................. $19.99

A YOUNG PIANIST'S FIRST BIG NOTE SOLOS
Early to Mid-Intermediate
10 short solos perfect for a student's first recital: Clowns • Glass Slipper • Let's Waltz • The Little Shepherd • New Roller Skates • Pagoda Bells • Smoke Signals • Spooky Footsteps • Swing Your Partner • Water Lilies.
00416229.................................... $6.99

Many more collections, duets and solo sheets available by William Gillock. Search for these and more Willis Music publications for piano at willispianomusic.com.

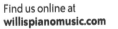

ABOUT THE COMPOSER

GLENDA AUSTIN was born and raised in Joplin, Missouri. She has vast experience as a church musician, beginning with her early years in the Baptist church, where she performed solos and improvised duets with her older sister Gloria on the organ.

Recently retired from a lifetime of general music teaching, Glenda continues to be a pianist for various chamber and concert choirs at Missouri Southern State University. Along with composing and arranging, she regularly hosts Facebook Lives from her living room piano. She also has an active YouTube channel that showcases her diverse piano styles.

Glenda received her music degrees from the University of Missouri at Columbia. She is married to David, her hometown high school sweetheart, and they enjoy spending time with their family.